W9-BYL-123

WORLD'S WORST NATURAL DISASTERS

THE WORLD'S WORST
AVALANCHES

by Tracy Nelson Maurer

CAPSTONE PRESS
a capstone imprint

Blazers Books are published by Capstone Press,
1710 Roe Crest Drive, North Mankato, Minnesota 56003
www.mycapstone.com

Library of Congress Cataloging-in-Publication Data is available
on the Library of Congress website.
ISBN: 978-1-5435-5481-6 (library hardcover) — 978-1-5435-5905-7
(paperback) — 978-1-5435-5485-4 (eBook PDF)

Summary: Learn about the world's most historic avalanches.

Editorial Credits
Gena Chester, editor; Juliette Peters, designer; Jo Miller,
media researcher; Tori Abraham, production specialist

Photo Credits
AP Images: Str, 16–17; Dreamstime: Brett Pelletier, 26; Getty Images:
AAron Ontiveroz/Contributor, 24–25, Jack Fletcher/Contributor, 14–15,
Library of Congress/Contributor, 10–11, Roberto Schmidt/Staff,
18–19, SHAH MARAI, 12–13; Mary Evans Picture Library: Illustrated
London News Ltd, 20–21; Newscom: Danita Delimont Photography,
27; Shutterstock: leonello calvetti, Cover, 3, 31, My Good Images,
Cover, 4–5, Piotr Snigorski, 29; SuperStock: Clickalps SRLs/age
fotostock VFI-2792927, 22–23, Exactostock-1598, 8–9, World
History Archive, 6–7

Design Elements
Shutterstock: Ivana Milic, Lysogor Roman, xpixel

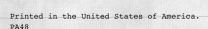
Printed in the United States of America.
PA48

TABLE OF CONTENTS

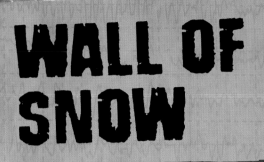

WALL OF SNOW

After days of heavy snowfall on the mountain, sunshine warms the air. Suddenly a huge slab of snow loosens. The wall of snow slides down the slope. Run! It's an **avalanche**!

Ice, rock, **debris**, and snow are all types of avalanches.

avalanche—a mass of snow, rocks, ice, or soil that slides down a mountain slope; avalanches are also called snow slides

debris—piles of rock fragments and loose, natural materials

ANIMAL DISASTER

Location:
The Alps, Italy

Date:
218 BCE

Lives Lost:
About 18,000

###

= 1 thousand people

More than 2,000 years ago, a North African army was crossing into Italy through the **Alps**. Horses and elephants carried their gear. The elephants' heavy footsteps on fresh snow set off avalanches. About 18,000 men died.

Avalanches happen for many reasons. Rapidly warming temperatures and extreme weather are common causes.

Alps—a large mountain range in Europe

DANGER ZONE

Location:
Andermatt,
Switzerland

Date:
Winter of
1950–1951

Lives Lost:
240

###

= 1 hundred people

Andermatt, Switzerland, faced heavy snowfall during the winter of 1950–1951. The weather caused a series of avalanches. On January 20, six avalanches roared down the Alps. They caused massive destruction and killed 240 people.

FACT Since 1936, more than 2,000 people have died in avalanches in Switzerland.

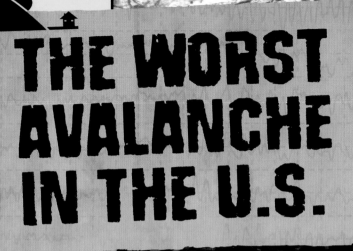

THE WORST AVALANCHE IN THE U.S.

Location:
Wellington,
Washington, USA

Date:
March 1, 1910

Lives Lost:
At least 96

\#\#\#\#\#
\#\#\#\#\#

\# = ten people

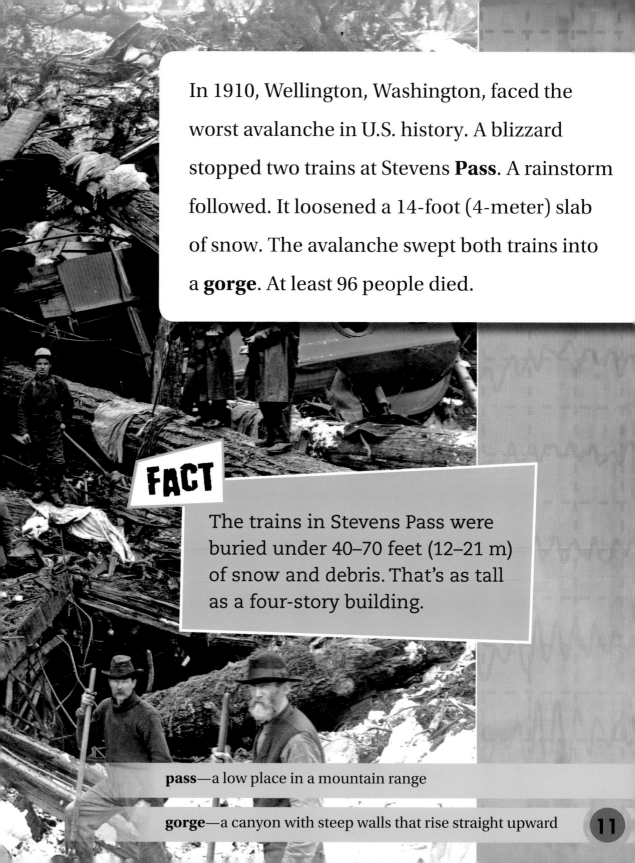

In 1910, Wellington, Washington, faced the worst avalanche in U.S. history. A blizzard stopped two trains at Stevens **Pass**. A rainstorm followed. It loosened a 14-foot (4-meter) slab of snow. The avalanche swept both trains into a **gorge**. At least 96 people died.

FACT

The trains in Stevens Pass were buried under 40–70 feet (12–21 m) of snow and debris. That's as tall as a four-story building.

pass—a low place in a mountain range

gorge—a canyon with steep walls that rise straight upward

RISKY ROADWAY

Location:
Salang Pass,
Afghanistan

Date:
February 9, 2010

Lives Lost:
More than 170

##

= 1 hundred people

On February 9, 2010, 17 avalanches rumbled through Salang Pass in Afghanistan. The snow buried cars, trucks, and buses. It also clogged a tunnel. Thousands of people were trapped inside. More than 170 people died.

Rescue workers ended up saving around 3,000 people in Salang Pass.

KILLER ICE

Location:
Andes Mountains, Peru

Date:
May 31, 1970

Lives Lost:
About 25,000

\#\#\#\#\#
\#\#\#\#\#
\#\#\#\#\#
\#\#\#\#\#
\#\#\#\#\#

\# = 1 thousand people

In 1962, an ice avalanche on Mount Huascarán, Peru, destroyed several villages. At least 3,500 people died. Eight years later, an avalanche of rock and snow struck the same area. The disaster killed about 25,000 people.

RUSSIAN RUIN

Location:
North Ossetia,
Russia

Date:
September 20,
2002

Lives Lost:
More than 100

+

= 1 hundred people

In 2002, near North Ossetia, Russia, a large chunk of ice broke off a **glacier**. It sped down a mountain, spurring an avalanche. The ice, water, and rock buried the town of Nizhny Karmadon. More than 100 people died.

FACT

Another glacier broke off near North Ossetia in 1902. It caused a smaller avalanche than the 2002 disaster.

glacier—a huge moving body of ice that flows down a mountain slope or across a polar region

NO ESCAPE

Location:
Mount Everest,
Nepal

Date:
April 25, 2015

Lives Lost:
At least 19

#####
#####
#####
####

= 1 person

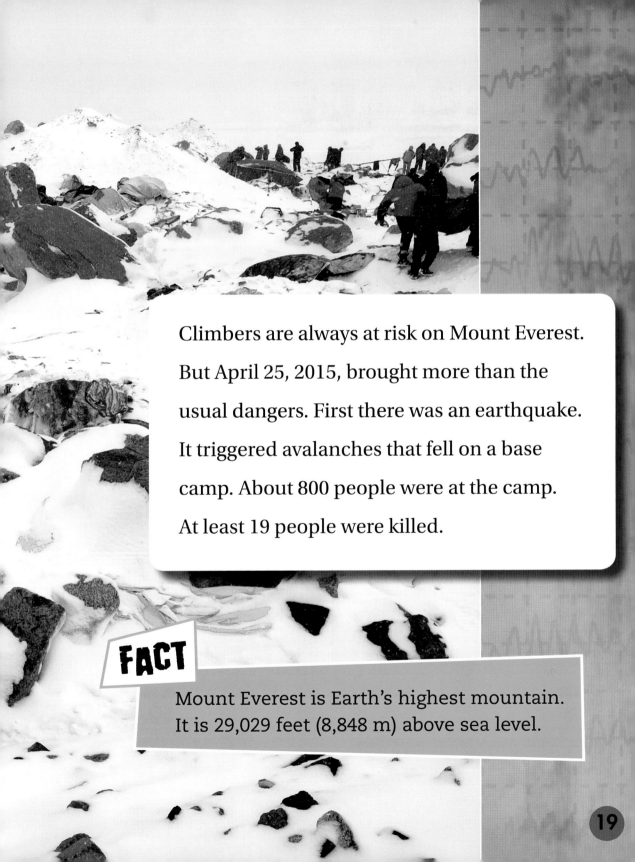

Climbers are always at risk on Mount Everest. But April 25, 2015, brought more than the usual dangers. First there was an earthquake. It triggered avalanches that fell on a base camp. About 800 people were at the camp. At least 19 people were killed.

FACT

Mount Everest is Earth's highest mountain. It is 29,029 feet (8,848 m) above sea level.

AVALANCHE ATTACKS

Location:
Tyrolean Alps,
Italy

Date:
Winter of
1916–1917

Lives Lost:
About 18,000

\#\#\#\#\#
\#\#\#\#\#
\#\#\#\#\#
\#\#\#

\# = 1 thousand people

During World War I (1914–1918), Italian and Austrian armies in the Alps used avalanches like bombs. **Explosives** and heavy snow triggered a series of avalanches one winter. Some 18,000 soldiers were killed by the snow.

FACT

Bodies caught in avalanches during World War I were still being found 80 years later.

HERE, THEN GONE

Location:
Plurs, Switzerland

Date:
September 4, 1618

Lives Lost:
Between 1,500 and 2,500

-
###

= 1 thousand people

The village of Plurs, Switzerland, once sat in the shade of a mountain. The town disappeared in one day. A powerful avalanche swept away everything in its path. Between 1,500 and 2,500 people died.

FACT

Only one building survived the Plurs avalanche. Today it is surrounded by orchards and farmland.

BACKCOUNTRY RESCUE

Location:
Cameron Pass,
Colorado, USA

Date:
March 2, 2013

Lives Lost:
1

\#
___
\# = 1 person

Four skiiers were in Colorado's Cameron Pass when an avalanche hit. Two, Alex White and Joe Philpott, were buried in the snow. Philpott did not survive. Park rangers eventually found White buried. They dug for three hours and pulled him out alive!

FACT

Most avalanche victims survive if they are dug out within 15 minutes. White only had a 1 percent chance of survival.

Alex White

AVALANCHE PROTECTION

Avalanches happen in all mountain areas. To help protect people and towns, officials cause avalanches on purpose. That way they can control where snow flows so it causes less damage.

FACT

Some towns have built avalanche **barriers** from wood, metal, or concrete.

barrier—a bar, fence, or other object that prevents things from entering an area

SNOW SAFETY

Skiers, hikers, and snowmobilers should check snow conditions often. These tips can help you if you're caught in an avalanche:

1. Move your arms as if you're swimming to the surface.
2. Shout out so that people nearby know you're being swept away.
3. If buried, cup your hands over your mouth to create an air pocket for breathing.
4. If buried, poke your arms, a pole, or anything above the snow to alert rescuers.

GLOSSARY

Alps (ALPS)—a large mountain range in Europe

avalanche (A-vuh-lanch)—a large mass of ice, snow, or earth that suddenly moves down the side of a mountain

barrier (BAR-ee-ur)—a bar, fence, or other object that prevents things from entering an area

debris (duh-BREE)—piles of rock fragments and loose, natural materials

explosive (ik-SPLOH-siv)—a weapon designed to blow up after reaching its target

glacier (GLAY-shur)—a huge moving body of ice that flows down a mountain slope or across a polar region

gorge (GORJ)—a canyon with steep walls that rise straight upward

pass (PASS)—a low place in a mountain range

READ MORE

Johnson, Terry Lynn. *Avalanche!* Survival Diaries. New York: Houghton Mifflin Harcourt, 2018.

Lake, G. G. *Take Your Pick of Survival Situations.* Take Your (Equally Horrible) Pick! North Mankato, Minn.: Capstone Press, 2017.

Suen, Anastasia. *Avalanches.* Devastating Disasters. Vero Beach, Flor.: Rourke Educational Media, 2015.

INTERNET SITES

Use Facthound to find Internet sites related to this book.

Visit www.facthound.com.

Just type in 9781543554816 and go!

Super-cool stuff!

Check out projects, games and lots more at
www.capstonekids.com

CRITICAL THINKING QUESTIONS

1. Name three things that can cause an avalanche.

2. How could an avalanche happen in the summer?

3. Why is it important to cup your hands over your mouth if you become buried in snow?

INDEX